I hope someho
That it causes creas_____ ,
Whether they fall in brow or cheeks,
I hope the movement
is a reminder
that you are still malleable.
Perhaps at some time
you'll find a line in your mind
like a £10 note in the pocket of an old coat
and maybe it'll buy you a little clarity.

Alternate Endings

With love and stories,

Erin
xxx

Erin Bolens

Burning Eye

BurningEyeBooks
Never Knowingly
Mainstream

Supported using public funding by
ARTS COUNCIL
ENGLAND

This edition published by Burning Eye Books 2020

www.burningeye.co.uk

@burningeyebooks

Burning Eye Books
15 West Hill, Portishead, BS20 6LG

ISBN 978-1-911570-86-8

Alternate Endings

CONTENTS

STARTS

TRIGGER WARNING

This dream contains images you may find upsetting
and some you wish you had forgotten.
There will be nudity you weren't expecting
that may or may not be flattering;
it will have nothing to do with lighting.
There will be flash feelings,
smoking, and let's not rule out gunshots.
Some scenes will be inexplicably mundane
and therefore unsuitable for younger dreamers.
Please take this as a trigger warning for everything
you have ever felt, imagined feeling or seen
with your eyes open or closed.
If you require further information,
walk backwards with the lights on.
If you require assistance, ask yourself kindly.
You will find feedback forms behind your teeth.
The dream will continue in the next

WORRY DOLL I

I worry about not doing enough exercise, so I go swimming. I worry that because I don't do enough exercise my swimming is too slow for someone of my age, health and capability. I worry that the lifeguards are judging me. I worry they might suggest ways I can improve my technique. I worry they might ask why I am slow. In case this happens (this has never happened), I decide that I will say I am recovering from an injury – probably a torn ligament in my shoulder – and that not being able to swim faster is really frustrating. I worry that if I say this it will lead to questions and conversations around shoulders and ligaments that my limited biology knowledge will not support. If this happens, I will say that I think it was a torn ligament, but I was too busy to get a diagnosis, so I'm just easing myself back into my very sporty life with some gentle swimming. Triathlon next. I make a mental note to never mention the word triathlon. Not even as a joke. There is no scenario that would end well if I ended up having to do a triathlon to prove a point. It would kill me.

WHY

after Sharon Olds

My mother is the only picture of my grandparents
together.
I never saw their faces as the tops of bodies,
the strike and spark of so much pain.

She sees herself now   as the reason for it all,
why a tornado had to impregnate a sleeping town,
leave a nine-year-old head featherless
with too many questions,
why lives were threatened and ended
without any talk of love.

She sees herself now   as a happy thing,
something useful that for whatever reason
would not have happened without fire.

PLANETS

Astrologically speaking, she says,
the rough roads are par for the course.
Mars is in retrograde;
no one can escape.
A throwaway comment
if it weren't for the pamphlet she's made
outlining stars with highlighters,
good will and a confidence so strong

my eyes become embarrassed
to be so earthbound
while she has the whole sky labelled,
colour-coded, backdated,
finding answers in the atmosphere to
questions no one remembers asking.

No risks this week, ey?
Maybe avoid sharp objects too.
I'll try, I say. And I do,
but even the cautious fan gets hit by shit
and somehow she's expected it –
leaping from life's long grass
with a rape alarm and a lasagne,
hand cream in the post,
teabags and notes,
flowers bought with invisible coins
to convey messages already written
in wrinkles I read in the mirror.

On the flip side – those well-starred days,
those lucky trines – she glows
like a sun not yet discovered,
bleaching my doubts with its shimmer.
I don't know about planets like her.
I can name a handful, draw less,
but I see the whole solar system
dancing above her head.

When I picture them spinning
when she isn't here,
the little one drops out of the sky
and sets up a world in my throat
that I will never swallow.
Mars is in retrograde; just be careful, love.
Mum, I don't think he's the only one.

WILLOW

By the time we buried her it was raining.
Not sheet rain but enough to feel clichéd.
She was dead when *The Archers* was on
but I didn't know. The episode played out
before I saw the little body, all velvet fur
and bloody nose. I was bouncing on the sofa,
my parents packing up the miniature cereal boxes
that have always meant *holiday*. I'm not sure where
April Fools' Day fits in, but I have to mention it,
don't I? A prank that wasn't funny and came too late.
It doesn't count after midday, I didn't say.
I don't remember the first cat dying.
I don't remember the weather, or the box,
or carrying on with a belly full of earth.

OVERSHARING AT THE HAIRDRESSER'S

In the interest of honesty I tell her
I'm going to visit my dad's grave
up a mountain overlooking a lake,
not a revelation   just how
September goes. Janet isn't fazed,
asks *when* and *why* and *how*,
gets hung up on age,
weighs mine and my brother's
with confident scales.

Harder for him   she says,
at that age   for a boy
at that age   much harder.
I nod because of the mirror.
Easy when you're young   isn't it?
You don't know what's going on.
Her scissors are a lot slower
than her tongue –
nearly two hours for a trim.
It is thick, yes, but

how does she fit everyone in?
With her slow-motion snipping
and chair that refuses to swallow me
even when I plead.
She holds up the little mirror
for me to view my head
from a different angle
and I see two children
piling earth on top of bones
at the nape of my neck.

OLDER, SIX YEARS, YEAH, WE DO, YEAH

It took me decades to be okay
with liking things you don't like
or disliking things you do.

There are no films about how we became
people who can speak and count and see
so sometimes I watch the boxset of you
to cut myself a little slack.

You threw yoghurt in my hair once   you are
the only person I know to have called me a cunt
but I would rather not have been born
than you not have been born.

Never twinned cities, our faces turned
into mirror balls after all   when I catch you
in the light   I see everything
that makes me glad.

YOU DIDN'T WHAT?

You remember at school when?

It's a legs-stretched space-hogger of a topic
I squish into tiny bottles kept at the bottom
of my bag. A strong scent that your stories
get lost in. Tell me what you wrote on those notes,
how you made that supply cry,
that time at the back of the bus
or behind the bins. I want to feel these things.

Did you have lessons in your pyjamas, then?

I've never worn a tie,
bells rang a different language,
I don't have a relationship with corridors.
I think I mostly got dressed –
but weren't all clothes pyjamas in the nineties?
There aren't many certificates with my name on.
I probably heard about it on Radio 4.
I don't know; there's no way I can know that.

Did you used to, you know, at school?

I am at the gates looking in.
You are playing those hand-clapping games;
I am an alien.
You are eating lunch on timetables;
my knowledge is a question mark.
You have twenty-nine brilliant friends that really get you;
I am making Beanie Babies as interesting as they can be.
It's impossible to know the nature of the courtyard
from this side of the bars.

When you were at school, did you?

Yes. Maybe. Long story. It depends, doesn't it?

CONGRATULATIONS

for getting on with it all –
for eating cake and doing sums
at the table your dad's body lay on.
For making tea and choosing funeral shoes,
for just taking it all in and only once
a couple of years on   lying on the floor
to scream.

There should be stickers for these things.
There should be cards to say well done
for walking past three of your alternate endings
in the street   without losing it,
without peeling *what-ifs* off the pavement
and stuffing them in your mouth to try to taste
looser spit.

Trophies should be awarded for replying politely
to pointless emails on the days you remember
what a dead body looks like –
on mornings when you wake and for a second
the dream is still real and your dad
is going to pop round later and fix that door
or at least try.

WORLDS

WORRY DOLL II

I worry about my effects on the environment. I decide to stop using tampons and pads. I Google menstruation cups. That's a minefield. There are different sizes. And shapes. I don't know what size or shape my vagina is. I've never really seen it that way; no one has ever told me. It appears important to know how high your cervix is. I'm not entirely positive I'm 100% sure which bit the cervix is. I worry I don't know enough about my vagina. I worry my lack of knowledge about my vagina is impacting negatively on the environment.

I Google how to find the height of my cervix. I instantly regret that. I worry about my internet browsing history. I always worry about my internet browsing history. I worry that they will scour it after I'm dead and draw false conclusions from the number of times I visited people's social media profiles. I worry that if I delete my internet history it will look like I have something to hide. Which I do. But it's a slight obsession with what so-and-so is up to or what what's-her-name looks like now and a semi-genuine belief that I might be able to solve high-profile missing persons cases with a few sage Google searches. It's nothing sinister. But if I delete it, it might look like that, mightn't it? Best to leave it, then. Live with it, die with it.

DEALS WITH NATURE

I know that some of the animals
I could have eaten were probably pricks.
They are not in a field making a shrine to me
because I didn't dip them
in mayonnaise at their funeral.

The polar bears don't know
that I am trying to use less plastic,
the orangutans can't know
I'm buying different biscuits,

the cows won't be told
when I turn down profiteroles,
the fish won't celebrate
a year since I used a face wipe.

On the days that I do nothing
but deplete the earth's resources
I am glad that we never
taught nature resentment,

that the trees are completely indifferent
to who benefits from their oxygen.

WE'RE ALL POETS IN THE QUIET COACH, AREN'T WE?

Everything feels like it belongs in a poem
when viewed from a train window.
I have been imposing melancholy
on sheep and barns for years,
with no plans to stop.

I know the pylons are not tightropes,
the clouds don't resent me,
the horizon is not a deadline,
the birds are not ink blots,
the trees are not punctuation,
the sunsets are not wise
or the houses weary,

but there is something
about speeding through it all
in a warm tube that turns the rain
into metaphors
sliding down the window
looking for an in.

WORRY DOLL III

I worry that my housemates are shit at recycling. I worry they will think I am a killjoy if I tell them they are shit at recycling. Even if it's in a nice way. (Is there a nice way?) I worry about my lack of authority. I worry that my lack of authority is having a negative impact on the environment.

RIVER

More purpose than a lake.
Less ambition than the sea.
More romance than a road.
Well, no one has Friday drinks
by the M1, do they?
No one has a favourite set of traffic lights
or goes for picnics on a dual carriageway.
I never stop and pause just to listen to cars
or wave to people on bridges when I'm driving.
I certainly wouldn't pay for a round trip in a taxi
just for fun.
What is it about watching water?
What do we withdraw from riverbanks
that has us always coming back?

RIVER POLICE

The police boat passes;
they wave.
I hesitate and wave back.
This has never happened before.
Later, feeling inspired,
I wave to a police car in Lewisham.
The event is not repeated.

SO A MESS, THEN

When anyone is described as
best in their field
I picture them quivering when they are
absolutely anywhere else.

WORRY DOLL IV

I worry I will run out of phone battery. So I take a power bank. I worry that might break, so I take two. I worry someone else might need a power bank but have a different phone, so I take three cables. Every time I leave the house. Sometimes I worry they will think I am strange for having a cable I don't need, so I stop myself from offering my power bank. I worry about how much water or electricity or how many tired hands it took to make my power bank. I think maybe I should learn to read an actual map. And to bloody relax. I worry that my lack of ability to read maps and to bloody relax is having a negative impact on the environment.

TRYING TO MIND MY OWN BUSINESS THE DAY AFTER MY YOUNG PERSON'S RAILCARD RAN OUT

The student was laughing at a croissant
at the counter and I wanted to cry.
I didn't hear what it said
but it was filled with ham and cheese
and was clearly hilarious.

She wore her coat just on her shoulders
as if it was a cape
or her arms were too heavy to reach the sleeves;
perhaps someone had said that is chic.

Her friend made the barista give him
samples of a few different coffees,
swilled them round like wine.
I heard the words *fruity* and *fragrant*
drift over his quiffed ego.

She giggled when he said,
I'm a coffee snob – guilty.
They asked for takeaway cups
even though they sat down at a table.
I bet their recycling bin is a car crash.

He said, *Very nice coffee, actually,*
with a tone of surprise
that made me cough up my crisps.
I don't know who I pitied more –

these friends who were strolling along
as if there was only ever one option
or me   the ghost of their future yet to come,
nine years their senior
and no longer easily amused by pastries.

WORRY DOLL V

I worry that people will think I am just giving to my friends' charity fundraising pages to look like a good person, so I do it anonymously. Then I worry that people will be wondering why I haven't donated to their charity fundraising pages. I worry about my need to please people. I worry that my need to please people is having a negative impact on charity fundraising.

Hearts

À LA CARTE

What do you fancy? the waiters say.
This lot are diligent   well trained,
they know the specials and the soup,
they've sniffed me out, they know I'm new.
We have a lovely beard on the menu today,
one suggests
Do you like beards? I pause. Close my eyes,
picture a forest of chins and nod.
Yeah. Yeah, I could have a beard.

She brings a six-foot-tall beard to my table.
The shaping is exemplary,
the conversation minimal,
a second date is unlikely,
a relationship would be problematic.
Meet my beard! I would say at parties,
Sorry, I can't come tonight;
I'm spending time with my beard.

I do what I never do in restaurants
and send it back. *Misunderstanding, sorry.*
Okay. It's not to everyone's taste.
How about glasses? she persists.
Or tattoos? Ooh, we have a fine flannel shirt…

I leave the table quietly,
bumping into a pair of five-foot-ten Ray-Bans
on my way out.

ARE YOU SEEING ANYONE?

a quartet of haiku
(four pretentious sentences)

i

If you leave post sex
with just an email address –
he's probs not the one.

ii

I think you might be
worth the inevitable
urine infection.

iii

If he leaves post-sex
with your Oyster card he is
also not the one.

iv

If you describe your
type as boy next door, you have
not met my neighbours.

WEDNESDAY COULD WORK

The Northern line is down and I need a wee.
I slip in and out of McDonald's like it's a strip club.
We haven't met and I want it to end well.
Like all of those lambs I fed to be eaten,
I hold things firmly, with care. *Bus or walk?*
I want to go home so much I forget trains exist.
Take me home. Turn the big light off.
We will never Google all of the questions or ages
of celebrities; let's agree they're a bit older now
like us. Open the window, bring yourself back.
Unlearn the teenage years.
Someone on the line at Euston, I message
but you're already here.

SEEING LONDON

I call London my fling,
but we are now five years in
and even I'm not buying that anymore.
London is not my type.
I never thought I would find
this level of self-confidence attractive.
I tell people we barely see each other,
but my clothes are strewn across his floor,
I've had a toothbrush in his loo for years.
Friends say, *You and London, you're a thing, then?*
I say *no*, mysteriously, *not really, not seriously.*
They look confused.

They ask me about Leeds.
I say, *We're still in touch,*
he's still the one,
we'll be married one day, I say,
we just want different things
but we'll snap back, just like that,
it's sort of what we do.
I say it like I know it's true,
but really I know Leeds is moving on.
He has new tattoos. New hair,
a new best mate called John Lewis,
and I'm desperately trying to see through this;
I don't know where I fit.
My anecdotes are out-of-date,
my small talk is patronising
and I never hear his news first-hand these days.

No one asks me about Manchester anymore.
They never understood that
but wished us well.
We needed each other for a bit;
he was my bit of rough; I was his safe bet.
We didn't last, didn't ask each other
enough questions for that.
I hope we meet at a party in a few years and smile.
Say *you look well* across the buffet and mean it.

Meanwhile, people send London and me
joint Christmas cards.
They say *how's London?* before *how're you?*
I don't know, I say defensively;
ask him yourself. They do.
They come back beaming from his side of the room –
he's so cool.
He told me about the new project –
the nightclub-cum-hospital-cum-avocado-farm-cum-café.
He's great. You're so lucky.
My smile is so forced
it nearly tears my face apart.
I know I have to break this up
before it breaks my heart, but...

When I get home
London has put theatre tickets on my pillow.
Spread them out in an attractive fan.
I try to resist but I'm not sure if I can.
That night, I have another dream of Leeds.
A dirty dream.
The Yorkshire moors all naked and speckled
with purple heather freckles.

In the dream I skip across fields
with a whippet I have never owned.
I sit in a picturesque pub I have never been to,
chat to rosy locals I have never met
in a tone I have never used.
Instead of a bath I climb
into a giant Yorkshire pudding
and submerge myself
in gravy that is definitely not vegetarian.
When I dunk my head under the film of fat

I wake up.
London is snoring in my ear,
arms around my waist,
spooning me so tenderly I want to cry.

I want to run back into the arms of the city
I have always called mine, but
Leeds hasn't called this year
and London is being… kind.
All right. I sigh. *All right.*
You win, London –
I like you. You make me laff.
And I drape myself around him like a scarf.

London raises a sleepy eyebrow and says,
C'mon, you know now, it's larf.

WORRY DOLL VI

I worry about using the tap if a housemate is showering. I worry about showering in case a housemate needs to use the tap. Sometimes I fill up the washing-up bowl and the kettle before I have a shower in case that's what they wanted the tap for. Sometimes I brush my teeth with water from my bottle if a housemate is in the shower. I am fairly certain they don't care about either occurrence, but I had to have an interview for the room, and anything that requires an interview makes me feel like I am on probation. It's been three years.

DIY

For almost too long I thought I'd be choosing
new paint pots with you.
Inevitable that we'd laugh at the names on tins
as we decided on the shade of things.
I thought once that we could have made a game

out of Homebase, but we knew
I'd ignore the ladders   focus on the snakes;
you'd start off willing   soon lose faith,
and we'd choose off-white anyway.

Better to remove these coats while we remember
the shape of our walls. Better not to play games
in shops that sell so many saws.

SPLIT

It came apart like the bruise
coloured smoothies I make,
fruit and water going
their separate ways,
two clean layers   no mistake,
no one wants to drink that,
do they, but a quick mix
could fix it   it hadn't spilt.

AVOIDANCE

When you face me I tell you about the ice cream parlour I used to plan trips to when I couldn't sleep: pack my bag meticulously, take enough change, decide which scoop would follow which sauce, which wafer would top it off, the compulsory cherry, a few nuts, eyelids droop.

That's beautiful, you say,

and I hope you are talking about Scarborough, about glasses taller than spoons, milk melting into fruit, women in yellow with soft scoop smiles serving children tucked under duvets at the counter, trying to drift off in a place that almost sounds like home. I realise I have eaten the time this bought; your glasses are off.

Yes, quite blind, you say,

and I wonder if you too have replaced this room with a sea view. It is 5 a.m. on this first floor in London, the parlour is years away, but I am ordering the whole menu as you draw me close, wondering how many Flakes it would take to make this taste familiar.

DIRTY TALK

I come out of the house to see the crow,
but the door isn't yellow
at this point. All four of us file out;
it's bigger than us,
the crow   I can feel that.

We position ourselves around the car
because it has to be moved
at some point.   As we bend
our knees for the lift   I tell him
I think this might be flirting.

WORRY DOLL VII

I worry about what the postman thinks of me because he almost always catches me in my pyjamas. Sometimes I quickly put lipstick on before I open the door so he might think I'm halfway through getting ready for a very important meeting.

Then I worry that he actually thinks I put lipstick on just to open the door.

I worry the postman thinks I wait for him. In lipstick and a bathrobe. I worry about my need to appear important. I worry that my need to appear important is having a negative impact on the postman.

ROUTE OPTIONS

When you lean on my shoulder
I see the new bar they have opened
on the top of your head,
red leather seats and old suitcases
bought online for a million pounds,

one of those old-fashioned places
that were popular sometime between
1604 and 1999,
intimate and easy to clean.
I don't breathe out for two weeks;
the windows cloud over anyway.

Your head is in the snug of the pub
on my collarbone.
What a homely spot, you say,
and I wonder what your place is lacking
for you to have wandered in here
and eaten all the crisps.

I write my shoulder's postcode
on a beer mat   hoping next time
you will use the shortest route,
come after hours   lie down   laugh
about the last time   like last time.

The landlady in my sternum chuckles,
says you stumbled in
when you were bursting,
pours you pints of everything,
cursing the catch on the door.

DETOUR

your house

a year on in the same spot
has not incinerated itself grown legs and run
or become remarkable at all I did check
at a distance like a warning or a weathered fox
squinting to see the eyeballs I left in the hedge
new gauges in your window neither appeared
no one tried to mug to me so I walked home
no fingerprints on the doorbell alibi in my open palms
it's on my way pretty much on my way as the

crow flies

WANT

after Kim Addonizio

I noticed it most with the man whose bed was in the living room,
an in-breath from the coffee table, two from the sofa, pushed
against the wallpaper we laughed about
before he drank all the water and asked me to spit,
before I started noting where the taps are in strangers' houses,
it was there the whole time – the want
to acknowledge all the lines and folds
that separated us   to say *you will not find porcelain*
here, I know it was not form that pulled you in,
but I hadn't worked out how to communicate shock
at something out of place whilst looking at a printer
with an open mouth in a room not made for a bed.
As the arm pressed down harder the printer spat for me,
spewing out pages covered in pictures of times I had been glad
and before I let the breath out, I saw the time I ran
towards my parents at the end of the festival
and thought *maybe the world is okay*
and *everything is great* and *aren't I lucky*
and it might have been because we were on holiday
or because my brother could have died
or because my dad hadn't yet
and it might have been because I had absolutely no reason
to think it possible that I wouldn't say
if I didn't like something
or because I was mostly made of stories at that point,
but it was the beginning
of taking pictures of feelings, of storing up
these big world thoughts to send to a printer
I would face one night in a room not designed for sleep,
with a man who didn't notice
all of these new expressions covering the floor,
dropping on top of Jack Kerouac's *On the Road*,
which I would have made so much fun of
if there had been breakfast,
if there had been any sort of looking back,
or looking down or labelling of things that did not belong.

WANTLESS

I looked for it with the man who said he was
looking for someone to talk to who wasn't
his mother. Haven't decided what colour flag that is.
I caught a glimpse of it in the taxi, but that's too early,
isn't it? Like a birthday party at the beginning
of a murder mystery. By the time we were in the room
with the green wall it had gone. I half-looked for it
down the side of the sofa while watching
a programme about Sunderland FC, enjoying it
the way you might like sitting in a car wash.

I scanned the room with the ironic photographs;
it wasn't there. Right when I might have been able
to acknowledge the folds and lines I try to iron out
in mirrors, there was no reason in my throat, my palms,
my toes, and maybe it was because of the broken finger
or because it had been that sort of year or because
I didn't finish the Red Stripe or because my purse
was stolen or because I knew there would be breakfast,
but it would be the same sort of excitement you get
about eating something leathery in a service station.
We should go now in case there isn't another for a while,
I need a wee, meet you by the fridge.

WANTED

He is building a sandcastle, giving in to a cigarette,
singing everything to the tune of 'Love Shack'.
I am rooting around in my bag, checking the football
against all odds, want is an aspirin under my tongue.

I'm not a big enough fish for regret   but if they ever
invent the thing   I will send his face back in time
to the printers of men with punctuation for eyes.
I'll send that creased smile   faux surprise   furrowed brow.

And maybe I, maybe they, would see it and know
that we are looking for the expression you can turn to
if the sun doesn't come up, if you need the whole world
to be built again quickly, without questions.

I BET THAT YOU LOOK GOOD ON THE PARK FLOOR (GRASS)

I've been picturing you in flip-flops.
I know we are in the slow-blink
gradual-stretch first-steps early-days stage,
but I have imagined you in shorts
moaning about the heat of the Tube.

I have absolutely mind-perved on the image of us
on a picnic rug, crumbs everywhere, many dips.
I think you might have opinions on barbecues
and mayonnaise. I bet your potato salad
would make me weak at the knees.

You've been walking around my August all week.
I've been smiling at you pushing back sweaty hair
from here in spring, wondering if August me
has dared to picture a November us,

you making a terrible bonfire pun
after I say something pretentious about leaves,
both of us as warm as you can be without burning.

FOR ME IT IS

to mop your brow in the middle of the night
with a damp flannel,
scrunching up days that don't have you in,

a shorter way of saying I will wait
until risk is a really high tide and swim anyway
in winter without a wetsuit,

of saying I am eating the bits of myself I used
to like the least because I am addicted
to the specific laugh
your specific silliness creates
in my throat,

a process of elimination that we all go through,
like when the doctor said my eczema is the type
they don't really have a name or cause for.

I'll use one word because we have settled
on democracy, the fair parent
we have learnt to respect
more than the acid in our stomachs.

DUNKABLE

It's a risk, isn't it? Submerging
biscuit in tea   bread in soup   me in new,
breathing in   hoping for better than tepid,
less than scald,
to soften   and rise before breaking point.

I was crumbling a bit there,
leaving bits of myself
at the bottom of mugs with shit slogans on,
hoping I'm still intact enough to be dunkable.

ENDS

WORRY DOLL VIII

I worry about going to the doctor's. I worry that I will either be wasting their time or too far gone to help. I worry which clothes I might have to take off. I always wear an elasticated waist to the doctor's. And a long top. A tunic affair is ideal. If I know I am going to have to take my bottoms off I worry about my under-the-tunic area. I try to work out what will look most like I haven't thought about it. Essentially I want my under-the-tunic area to convey to the doctor that I am organised and comfortable and that I definitely haven't prepared it aesthetically for an appointment. I never wear lace to the doctor's. I want to portray a cool, empowered, relaxed vibe. That isn't an option in salons or the M&S lingerie department. It would be easier if the options were bikini, Brazilian and smear test. I worry about my worrying about my under-the-tunic area. I worry that my under-the-tunic area is having a negative impact on the NHS.

HEATHCLIFF IS IN HIS THIRD YEAR AT DRAMA SCHOOL

and it's important that you realise
how tough that is.
As a mature student,
he doesn't believe in socialising
but can often be found saying
the academic assessment of art
is fucking bullshit
at dinner parties hosted by his lecturers.

He doesn't talk to the other students,
referring to them in his journal as cogs.
He has a name tattooed on his bicep
that everyone knows not to ask about.
He doesn't reply to messages on Tinder
because he's only on there for research.

His dissertation project
is a devised verbatim piece
exploring how trees communicate
their desire for violence.
You're not invited
but your presence is expected,
if not desired.

SUGAR PLUMS AND SWANS

The film you're trying to download has already finished.
It has been chewed and spat out, reviewed, parodied,
dated, sequelled, awarded, praised and remade.
It has ended so many times before it even buffers.
You are resurrecting something from your sofa

like when I imagine reading a book my mum
got from a charity shop to a child I haven't conceived,
like turning the television off before you see the score,
like putting your fingers in your ears whilst the people
on the train talk about that dramatic season finale.
It has ended. The finale. Ended when it was thought

and written and performed and filmed and shown.
But you wait. You wait to begin. We tap the shell
of endings every day, tentatively, with our little spoons,
finding a soft new middle in something someone would call
boiled. I have run smack bang into endings whilst calmly
saying I don't do them very well. I have convinced myself

an end is a sugar plum, like seeing an origami swan
in a crumpled receipt. I don't need sugar plums or swans
and neither do you. You do not have to begin to rise.
You do not have to end to melt.

DO WE HAVE TIME FOR MY TOP TEN THOUSAND?

I don't have a favourite, don't make me. If you push me off this fence, I will resent you. I like it here, this gentle realm where all the options serve me well. If you force me, I will pick and spend the rest of the day regretting it, the rest of the year realising how much the other options actually have to offer. I feel genuine pity for anyone that has ever said they have a favourite animal. Poor Emily with her 302 pig-shaped notepads and snout ice-cube tray and trotters flipping everywhere. John said he liked meerkats once – now his garage is a desert. Please don't make me draw a line in the sand that nothing can ever pass. I haven't tried all the cakes, I haven't read all the books – do not make me list things in an order I will respect for no longer than it takes me to say *David Attenborough, Judi Dench, Winnie-the-Pooh.*

I don't want a Leonardo DiCaprio keyring because I watched Titanic twenty years ago. I don't want a donkey duvet set because I once enjoyed a trip to a sanctuary. I am many things on different days; let me enjoy everything always and savour whatever little piece of now I have on my tongue.

If I have told you I have a favourite, I was probably lying. It's probably changed now, and telling everyone my new hierarchy of ice cream flavours or colours or friends would make an odd group email:

Dear everyone,
I know I once declared mint choc chip to be king,
but I've recently started really appreciating vanilla.
Yeah, I think it is an age thing. Send all.

If I'm doing that I should also ask about their lives and their favourite things, and that is a lot of admin – so best not to pick at all. Let me say all of them, let me say it changes, let me say purple for now, Earl Grey at the moment, let me move on if I need to, let me be open to every next thing being the best. For a bit.

AND ALL OF THE HUMANS WE'VE MET

after Lisel Mueller

Time is a massive train,
all steam and tracks and chance.
I can meet you at the station
because I was born at all
and I'm not dead yet.
Because I turned out to be me
and not a child Dickens wrote about
looking for love and food
in well-lit windows.
No one is chucking oranges at me
or standing by a river to see if I will float.
I wanted to be Florence Nightingale once
but I'm not, and on reflection
I'm probably glad.
I'm not Anne Boleyn either, thanking her neck
or Icarus's mother, hoping for rain.
I am packing your spare toothbrush,
smiling at double tickets
whizzing out of the machine,
amazed that you and I
and all of the humans we've met
have made it this far and ended up
in the same train carriage of time,
bone-achingly grateful to be able to buy
the coffee you like and watch it turn
your mouth into a phoenix.

WORRY DOLL IX

Some things are worth worrying about. Your worries are proof of your care, of your heart and your brain and your life. They are not an altar you must crumble at. Do not assume the cars will stop, look twice – that has always been a good idea. Check your symptoms with a real live person who has done the reading for you, that is good. Use compassion as a compass and don't always feel the need to pack your bag in preparation for every sort of natural disaster every time you leave the house. I am working on those ones. I am working on smiling at worry like a naff joke, on giving it the same amount of attention I give advertising or cold callers. I am making lists of things I used to worry about that melted, of things I might do with time I use to worry. I look at these lists and smile at time's sleight of hand. Then I worry I left off something very important.

POST-POEM ANALYSIS

This poem you've just given me,
given us,
where did you find it?
Was it sitting next to you on a train?
Did it ask you for change?
Was it yours?
A story hidden in handkerchiefs for too long?
Or was it borrowed from someone in too deep
to even think of describing the sea
they were drowning in?

Is it for me? To put in my pocket?
To change me?
Enrage me?
Melt me?
Accuse me?
Do you want it back?
Did you want me to clap?
Or click,
feel happy,
feel sick,
feel nothing?

Or was it for you?
So you'd feel better?
Connected?
Feel closure?
Respected?
So you'd feel
something?

I hope somehow it's useful.
That it causes creases in your face.
Whether they fall
in brow or cheeks,
I hope the movement
is a reminder

that you are still malleable.
Perhaps at some time
you'll find a line in your mind
like a £10 note in the pocket of an old coat
and maybe it'll buy you a little clarity.

THIS

Say that was the end,
how it all came together,

everything you got,
everything you did,

that was your lot.
An end that took a lifetime,

the details unknown until now
but inevitable as weather.

If that was the end then,
if that was the end then this,

this, or this – this
is the alternate bit.

SPACE FOR AN ENDING YOU HAVE
SOME SORT OF SAY IN

NOTES

'River' and 'River Police' were first published in *A Collection of River Inspired Poems*, created by the Thames Festival Trust as part of the Boat Poets project for Totally Thames Festival.

'Want' was commended in the University of Hertfordshire Single Poem Prize 2019 and published online.

ACKNOWLEDGEMENTS

Big thanks to…

The Burning Eye team for being so kind and encouraging and great at what you do. To Emma Hammond for the excellent questions and feedback on many of these poems. To Rachel Long for the brilliant workshops in which some of these poems started their life. To Carl for being someone I can show my early drafts to. To Mum and Lyall for the love and support always. To Dad for the beginning. To Mike for giving this book more happy poems than it was going to have.

9 781911 570868